Butter cups -

GARDEN SECRETS
of BUNNY MELLON

GARDEN SECRETS
of BUNNY MELLON

LINDA JANE HOLDEN, THOMAS LLOYD, AND BRYAN HUFFMAN

Foreword by P. Allen Smith

GIBBS SMITH
TO ENRICH AND INSPIRE HUMANKIND

CONTENTS

———

*T*o Bunny, with love.

Foreword

P. ALLEN SMITH

——

Creating a garden is a personal expression. One can tell much about the deeper make-up of a person by the gardens they create. Bunny Mellon was an extraordinary person in many ways. A person of great style, taste, all set within a full life of privilege, but with a love of the garden that grounded and shaped her throughout her life. I think the garden has a way of doing just that, doesn't it? Bunny learned early on that for those interested in gardens, nature would always meet you at least halfway. And, on that journey much about life—and oneself—can be discerned.

The collaboration between Linda Jane Holden, Bryan Huffman and Thomas Lloyd in *Garden Secrets of Bunny Mellon* is an important one, offering rare insights and lessons from the reserved Mellon. Although deeply private, Mellon was known as a great design talent and one of the 20th century's most celebrated style icons. Indeed, Mrs. Mellon and Mrs. Mellon's gardens continue to inspire today. *Garden Secrets of Bunny Mellon* offers us direct access to Mrs. Mellon's gardening passion, her process and her predilections vis-à-vis careful curation of her personal writings and photographs. This assembly has been attentively orchestrated by three personalities intimately familiar with her habits and design formulations. Each collaborator knew Bunny and her strong affection for garden design, each with a unique perspective to share.

Linda met Mrs. Mellon herself at Oak Spring, the Mellon family farm in Upperville, VA (a property with gardens I have long admired), when she went there to talk about gardening at the White House. What a conversation that must have been; and what incredible scholarship Linda was gifted, with direct guidance from Mrs. Mellon from her Oak Spring library—the very texts that Mrs. Mellon called upon to refine her own aesthetic and design technique.

Family and friends were a wellspring of warmth and joy for Mrs. Mellon, notably with her grandson Thomas Lloyd and, later in her life, with devoted personal friend and designer Bryan Huffman. From these gentlemen, we benefit from the perspective of kinship and kinship extended. Mr. Lloyd graciously navigated the Mellons' private collection and provided (much never previously made public) details of Bunny's private life, as well as his own loving recollections of Mrs. Mellon's work on family properties.

"Kissing Cousin" is the affectionate nickname Bunny had for Bryan. Southerners know this as a moniker reserved for the warmest of friends with whom secrets and thoughts are shared. As a friend of Bryan myself, I understand why he and Bunny became quick companions. I first met Bryan Huffman in his native North Carolina during a private party hosted by philanthropist and preservationist Tom Gray. Tom's notoriously well-preserved Philip Hoehns (now Hanes) home in Clemmons was the perfect background for a collection of design experts descending on historic Salem for the symposium of Early Southern Decorative Arts in 2018, of which I was the keynote speaker. Bryan shared with me then his love of the garden, design, and spirit of generosity. His close friendship with Bunny near the end of her life was filled with daily talks about design, projects, art, politics, gardens, and travel. Through these exchanges, Bryan became a steward of Bunny's mature and reflective design values, as well as her most memorable and personally rewarding design experiences. As Bryan testified to me, "It doesn't matter if one is in Virginia, Nantucket, Antigua or Paris—Bunny's style was Bunny's, her style is always identifiable and it is her own."

As an American whose own design ethos developed in Europe, I have a great admiration for Bunny's grounded approach to garden design and love of horticulture. And I also identify with her joy for experimentation and expression that were exercised at her many properties, just as I have at my Arkansas home, Moss Mountain Farm. She liberally borrowed from both the *jardin à la française* and *jardin à l'anglais* schools and rendered product with a distinct American accent.

During my formal education in England as a young man, I befriended similarly strong female tastemakers who contributed significantly to the landscape—"Debo" Duchess of Devonshire at Chatsworth, Nancy Lancaster at Little Haseley, and Viscountess Ashbrook at Arley, amongst others. Women such as Bunny from this postwar era were stylish, yet pragmatic. Imbued with a Jeffersonian spirit of a love of beauty, nature and functionality, Bunny crafted gardens that worked with nature, not against it. Meadow grasses and wildflowers allowed to go ungroomed in their natural state juxtaposed with more formal elements celebrated the art of the garden—and always with a bow to Nature herself.

Linda, Thomas and Bryan are to be applauded for their tireless work distilling Bunny's personal views and gardening techniques. Collecting these insights preserves skilled practical knowledge and cultural information of an important era in American gardening for everyone to access for generations to come.

The best gardeners are those with a long history in the garden and soil on their hands. Bunny was certainly both.

PREFACE

It was June 2010, and I had resumed previous talks about gardens with the White House gardener, Irvin Williams, whom I knew when I worked at the White House and who had recently retired. We were delving into the history of the Rose Garden. I mailed a letter to the Oak Spring Garden librarian requesting permission to view Mrs. Mellon's Rose Garden archives and he had responded by saying that Mrs. Mellon wanted to see me to discuss gardening at the White House when I came to Oak Spring, the Mellon family farm in Upperville, Virginia.

On the day of the visit, Bunny Mellon and I sat down together at a round table in her garden library in front of an immense and equally sunny Rothko painting that seemed to light up the space all around her. Straightaway she asked, "Linda, you worked in the White House. Which president did you work for?" Knowing of her friendship with the Kennedys, I suspected my honest reply would bring a hasty conclusion to our conversation and I would soon be on my way. But after answering that I had worked in the Reagan White House, I was surprised to hear her proclaim, "Oh! Ronnie was my second favorite president and Jack was my first."

In the White House I worked with the Assistant to the President for Administration, who had taken a keen interest in the gardens and grounds and wanted everything to be perfect. Our suite of offices was located on the ground floor of the West Wing, across the hall from the photographer's office, next door to the president's barber shop and down the hall and around the corner from the Situation Room. This is where I met Mr. Williams, who had come to work at the White House in 1961 to help Mrs. Mellon redesign the Rose Garden for President Kennedy. Gradually over those busy years of the Reagan Administration, Mr. Williams began telling me the story of the White House gardens and I soon realized that they, in actuality, were the gardens of Mrs. Paul Mellon, as Mr. Williams called her. He explained that Mrs. Mellon began her garden designs with what she called the "bones of the garden." In the Rose Garden she anchored the four corners of the plot with *Magnolia x soulangeana* (commonly called saucer magnolia) and intricately planted the connecting north and south flower beds with 'Katherine' crabapples centered in diamonds of santolina and surrounded by ribbons of box that zigzagged the length of the beds. The more I learned, the more I wanted to know.

After that June visit at Oak Spring, Mrs. Mellon opened her library to me and I began to spend a lot of time there reading her old garden books, which

I want to write a garden book but seem to lack time. It would be short. - A few suggestions that would encourage beginners and a few warnings - not to over do. - As the how you start you will change your ideas with experience. - If you are sincerely interested in the subject experience will carry you along. - sometimes with disappointment - but they too sharpen you & further your knowledge as you reach for a replacement or another approach. I would give a list of Books to have as reference. - In the dated back several centuries. A magical moment arrived when she invited me into her private walled garden. Upon entering through the old wooden gate, I remember thinking that this was how Mary Lennox must have felt when she stepped into the fabled Secret Garden. But unlike the hidden, neglected garden that Mary found, this garden was just as pretty as could be. Soft hues of pinks, lavenders, and blues hovered over sweeps of terraced flower beds that sloped to an arbor pleached with apple trees. Cordons of heritage varieties of pears, plums, and apples; old-fashioned flowers; prickly, hardy orange trees; and a panorama of espaliered enchantment filled the sight lines.

I continued my library visits up until her death, in March 2014, which was followed several months later by the Auction of the Decade in New York City, when most of Mrs. Mellon's possessions went on the auction block. The casual, informal country atmosphere that had seemingly permeated the old stone walls of the library had now given way to a cool and steely New York state of mind as the auctioneers filled their packing boxes. All of this had an adverse effect on me, and I began to seek solace in her garden journals, tarrying on her words and phrasing, absorbing the depths of her insight and understanding. I wished that someone would write a book about her gardening for gardeners like me—who wanted to know more—and fill it with fresh inspiration of how she did what she did,

descriptions of her planting schemes, advice, and remedies. Then the unexpected happened. As I was reading, I came across her sentence, "I want to write a garden book but haven't had time," and in that moment, I knew what had to happen: I must write that book for her. This is what initiated the research and writing for my first book, *The Gardens of Bunny Mellon,* and then a collaboration with Bunny's dear friend Bryan Huffman and her grandson, Thomas Lloyd. Together our continued search for material led to the discovery of a stash of garden photographs taken by Bunny herself.

It is important to understand that for Bunny Mellon a great day at the farm involved a drive across the streams and around the orchards and across the meadows, and—with her unerring and practiced eye—snapping photographs of favorite scenes and settings she viewed along the way, both for her personal pleasure and for study. It is this photography, along with her journal writings, that mostly comprise *Garden Secrets of Bunny Mellon.* Some additional photographs have been added to round out the garden views and visual content.

Bryan, Thomas, and I are grateful for the tremendous privilege and opportunity to bring this historical collection of Mrs. Mellon's garden writings and, in many cases, her own garden photography, to life and hope that you, too, will find inspiration.

—LINDA JANE HOLDEN

INTRODUCTION

*"I want to write a garden book but haven't had time.
It would be short. A few suggestions that would
encourage beginners and a few warnings not to overdo."*

Bunny Mellon's personal legacy began in a garden, and it is here that she began to develop her horticultural standards. She wrote in the preface of *An Oak Spring Sylva: A Selection of the Rare Books on Trees in the Oak Spring Garden Library* that her earliest memory of the beauty and harmony of the natural world began "near a bed of tall white phlox in her godmother's garden," and it was this "towering forest of scent and white flowers" that became the "beginning of a ceaseless interest, passion and pleasure in gardens and books." For as long as she could remember, she'd never been without a plant or something growing. For Bunny, seeds were a "wonderment."

In 1916, when she was just six years old, Bunny asked her father, Gerard Lambert, for a plot of ground at Albemarle, their family estate in Princeton, New Jersey. Mr. Lambert had taken great interest in the gardens and hired the best landscape company of the day, the Olmsted Brothers, to tend the vast grounds. In response to his young daughter's request, a "handkerchief"-size plot of land was marked out and she began to toil in her own bit of earth, working things out for herself. She plopped a birdbath in the center, "borrowed" a rosebush from her mother's garden, and "just went from there."

Mr. Lambert recorded his admiration for his eldest daughter's abilities in his autobiography, *All Out of Step: A Personal Chronicle*: "She had exquisite taste and the most original mind of anyone I knew." And in describing the skill she displayed during the construction of her next project, a small playhouse she designed and built in the woods at Albemarle, he added, "She stood over the workmen every minute directing them." For Bunny, this was just the beginning. Despite the fact that she was not an educated botanist, horticulturist, or landscape gardener, she applied her trial-and-error method of cultivation—and succeeded.

Perhaps Bunny's earliest garden design other than at her home was during her high school years, when she embellished the scenery at her alma mater, Foxcroft, a girl's school in Middleburg, Virginia. And, with a team of gardeners toiling at her side, she continued to gain a plethora of experience as she helped design and create gardens around the world for her family and friends. These ran the gamut, from a postage stamp–sized plot to a French chateau landscape to a historical garden restoration; to Mellon family gardens with names like Carter Hall, Apple Hill, the Brick House, Oak Spring, Dune House, and King's Leap; to Hubert Givenchy's Manoir du Jonchet in the Eure-et-Loir department, southwest of Paris; the White House; and at her private residences in Paris and Nantucket.

Bunny was always willing to try new things, and when her exacting eye was not pleased, she was equally willing to tear things out—or apart—and move on. Her books and abundant hands-on learning experiences were her teachers and helped lead the way as she stepped into a world of her own. In *A White House Diary*, Lady Bird Johnson, who in 1964 asked Bunny to continue the work she had begun for President and Mrs. John F. Kennedy in the White House gardens, accurately described Bunny's ability as a "working at it kind of knowledge."

Bunny kept notes in blank journals. She wrote about what worked and what didn't, what to try again and what to forget. She logged in recipes for "growing mousse" (moss), sketched out color schemes for next summer's garden beds, and wrote notes for the book she wanted to write. With her sensitive insight, Bunny mused, "This is a story about a garden." It was meant to be a guide, a starting point for beginners, and to offer encouragement.

"Every garden has its own way of being, its own geographical location, atmosphere, soil, and climate—and it is these differences that dictate a world of possibilities and make a garden unique," she wrote. One must put "together the things of nature that correspond to the person" as well as to the place and environment, she counseled. Every garden she made, whether it was for herself or the president of the United States, honored these differences.

Bunny gleaned information about gardening and horticulture from writings through the ages. She found inspiration in the written word of Solomon, the wise Old Testament king, and referenced his descriptions of the natural world in I Kings 4:33: "He described plant life, from the Cedar of Lebanon to the hyssop that grows out of walls. He also taught about animals and birds, reptiles and fish."

Turning the pages of *Garden Secrets of Bunny Mellon* will be akin to going back in time and stepping into her very private and rarefied world to see her gardens as she saw them, read about her garden standards and methods of cultivation, learn the rules she followed and the rules she broke, see how she put things together and how she pulled them apart, and pick up a few of her tips that she learned along the way while seeking her own special brand of imperfect perfection.

The view west toward the Blue Ridge Mountains from Bunny's bedroom window.

Some of Bunny's Notes and Tips:

- *Allow plants to roam a bit—like flax, daisies, columbine, phlox—like clouds that float over an organized design.*

- *Paris garden marvelous. Lavender in tubs important. Trees kept as low as possible to hide the street.*

- *Order white and pale pink peonies—no dark red—for next year. Check roses. Put order in June this year.*

- *Scillas are blooming with crocus. Look lovely in apple orchard with white and pink lavender crocus. Trees being pruned. Much better job this year.*

- *Things essential to gardening must be kept in one place.*

- *Subscribe to horticultural, organic gardening magazines—and read reference books like this!*

- *A low cement wall with clipped boxwood planted in front makes a good raised bed and is a less expensive option.*

- *Strips of rawhide are the best thing for tying an espalier tree. It gives with the weather and rarely cuts the bark.*

- *Lilies are better planted in pots than in the garden. Mark lilies in gardens for winter so they won't be uprooted.*

- *Flowers for September in Virginia: zinnia, white cosmos, large sun flowers, nigella, Persian jewels, Queen Anne's lace.*

- *Put lots of salvia pitcheri under canvas at Basket House—last longer and blue is beautiful. Can withstand cold weather and frost.*

- *Antigua plants: black willow, white wood, white cedar, ficus, acacia, cinnamon, bay rum, myrtle lime, wild lime, mahogany.*

Pastel shades of allium and foxglove blossom in springtime beside the garden wall.

Garden Secrets of Bunny Mellon shines a light on that up-until-now-elusive mystique that enveloped her garden and the subtleties of harmony she created through her planting schemes—her witches in the garden—and reveals how one can define and attain their own personal garden standards.

This book contains many selections from her journals and a significant number of never-before-seen photographs that were taken by her. It is the kind of book you will want to open again and again, returning to a favorite photograph or a selection on one of Bunny's standards of garden design—determining horizons and composing sight lines; creating atmosphere; the value of light, space and form; espalier and tree pruning; the use of trees as sculpture; the importance of using materials that relate to the earth; and comments on her tools of choice.

The story will touch on her own bug-a-boos: "Beware of nurserymen," as she cautions not to "overbuy or overplant or use too much mulch." It will reveal her standards—or Little Herb Trees, as she liked to call them—slips of myrtle, rosemary, and thyme fastened to twigs and grown into tabletop trees; these were probably some of her most cherished possessions, and they took center stage in her garden. Cultivating, trimming, and pruning these pretty little gems brought her great joy throughout her life and have become the symbol of her standards.

And, finally, there is Bunny's attention to detail and her precious appreciation for the small creatures who shared the garden. She created hideouts and sanctuaries for the birds, rabbits, and chipmunks to use whether they were seeking refuge from the elements or protection from predators. Bunny scribed the daily habit of one "small frail bird":

"A song sparrow sings from early morn until night in a tree near my window. In this small throat so strong and trusting there seems to be a whole world of beauty."

Bunny will teach you how to bask in the happy thought that the garden is your stage—and yours is the leading role. She will encourage you to be bold. Be brave. Be willing to experiment—to try new things. She would want you to understand that as you begin to tackle this new way of thinking and doing in the garden, "you are starting out on an adventure, and that if you are not too ambitious in the beginning, and you succeed more than you fail, you will have found a great happiness in life." She did.

A watercolor titled *Six O'clock*, by Mellon family friend Bee Dabney, documents the bunny that visited the gardens frequently.

RACHEL LAMBERT MELLON'S STORY

"Being very small near a bed of tall white phlox in my godmother's garden . . . was the beginning of ceaseless interest, passion, and pleasure in gardens and books."

*O*nce upon a time there was a Bunny who gardened at the White House during an era that became known as Camelot. It was June 1961. A young and energetic John F. Kennedy, America's 35th president, and his wife, Jackie, had just returned from a trip abroad that included a visit to Louis XIV's sumptuous gardens at the Palace of Versailles. President Kennedy had been deeply moved by the carefully orchestrated diplomatic events—particularly the solemn moments in the garden framed by the stunning grandeur of the horticultural displays, light shows, and spiraling fountains. At the time, Bunny Mellon wrote in her journal that the president had keenly felt "the subtle influences of nature on the human mind" and had begun to realize that there was nothing that rivaled the botanical caliber of the French at the White House. Not surprisingly, it wasn't too long before Kennedy turned to his trusted friend, Bunny Mellon, the amateur gardener who had admitted to having "no experience in formal studies," and asked her to make an American garden for him at the White House.

This is a story about that amateur gardener, Bunny Mellon, who had "wanted to write a book about gardening but didn't have time." "Each day," she said, "it becomes more clear that I must write. The awareness of nature is a gift," and "one is never at a loss for pleasure."

This book is lavished with Bunny's own writings from her garden journals. It is filled with much of her own photography—pictures she snapped during her daily outings—her walks through the gardens and drives across the Mellon family farm in Upperville, Virginia. It reveals how she lived and gardened in the natural world.

Born in 1910 in New York City, Bunny Mellon created gardens for family and friends throughout her lifetime that spanned geographic locations from the warm waters of the Caribbean to the frosty shores of the Atlantic and the gentle, meandering rivers of France—each with its own climate and weather conditions, soil compositions, and ranks of native plants. She was a woman ahead of her time, in a time when terms such as *sustainable development, Tidy Towns, global warming*, and *climate change* had not yet become ubiquitous and raised an international awareness. Yet, even then, Bunny was aware of the delicate harmony of a coexistence that demanded the careful balancing of human needs and aspirations in conjunction with the use and enjoyment of the natural world. She and her husband, Paul Mellon, were actively committed to the conservation of natural landscapes and quietly contributed to sponsored initiatives by providing funds for acquisition of coastal lands, state parks, and natural areas for wildlife preserves that will benefit humankind in per-

petuity. These substantial efforts—the care and protection of vast acres of native lands—began, so simply, in a garden.

"My first awareness of the outside world, beyond the loving hands that surrounded me, was of being very small near a bed of tall white phlox in my godmother's garden. This towering forest of scent and white flowers was the beginning of ceaseless interest, passion, and pleasure in gardens and books. Like a magic carpet it has carried me through life's experiences, discoveries, joys, and sorrows. In sadness especially it has been a hiding place until my heart mended." Bunny "tried to save flowers by putting them in dog water bowls—anything to save them," and, to her mother's chagrin, rearranged the plants in her garden. Bunny noticed everything.

"Beginning with infants' rag books of colored pictures printed on coarse cloth, through all the books of early childhood, I was led on and on. I will never forget the illustrations and drawings of Beatrix Potter's greenhouses, flower pots, and potting sheds; Kate Greenaway's verses and books, in which fruit trees full of apples and pears hang over pale brick walls; Boutet de Monvel's precise drawings with the music of French nursery rhymes written across pictures of bridges, tall, square French houses, and trees planted in rows like soldiers. But of all these my favorite illustrator was H[enriette] Willebeek Le Mair.

Her pictures in *Songs of Childhood*, Robert Louis Stevenson's *A Child's Garden of Verses*, and other books were a young gardener's delight—walls, topiary trees, fruit arbors, sand dunes, and fields of wildflowers."

Picket-style garden gates that fastened with old iron latches; images of flowery vining plants with delicate tendrils that rambled across tidy garden paths and clung to the edges of dry-stacked stone walls; lily ponds where worn tin pails could be dunked and filled with water for splashing on leafy garden gems; and an abundance of wildflowers that speckled terraces and pathways formed with pieces of irregularly shaped stone also filled her imagination.

"Fairy tales followed, never to end, with illustrations including those of Arthur Rackham and Edmund Dulac—Rackham's gnarled oaks and apple trees, willows, and windswept hills, and Dulac's medieval turrets where ladies embroidered and planted carnations, roses, and herbs as men battled in the distant landscape."

Bunny "translated" these beloved scenes of enchantment into miniature gardens, first in a garden sandbox then later in seedling tray flats, knitting together bits of twigs and snips of leaves gathered under the apple trees and in the flower beds. Small plants lined her windowsills and she "gathered wildflower seeds as if they were gold found in streams."

Her grandfather, Arthur Houghton Lowe (1853–1932) gave Bunny her first flower book, *Flower Guide: Wild Flowers East of the Rockies* and "encouraged this enthusiasm." Grandfather Lowe led her "through woods and up mountains," taking her on trips to Concord, Massachusetts, "to learn and study the world of Alcott, Thoreau, Emerson, and Hawthorne." Her childhood home, Albemarle, in Princeton, New Jersey, was "surrounded by open fields" and, Bunny wrote, "Wildflowers were part of my feeling of freedom." Bunny noticed these rugged plants, sown by nature, dotting the fields and coloring the landscape like "a sea in the wind." She fondly remembered "seeing acres of yellow mustard and blue flax throughout Europe" and believed that "flowers are the paint box of garden design" and "can create a sense of peace and simplicity."

As a young adult, she admired the work of Lancelot "Capability" Brown, the great English landscape designer known for his ability to envision the "capability" of a landscape. He is remembered for his enhancement of natural landforms as he sculpted shapes and topographical forms into undulating lawns, edging tree-framed vistas with serpentine waterways that reach into the distance.

Bunny, a Francophile, paid close attention to two of Louis XIV's gardeners who worked to create the gardens and landscape at the Palace of Versailles. One, André le Nôtre, worshipped

LEFT: The King's Gate at le Potager du Roi, the Palace of Versailles, which was restored by Bunny and Paul Mellon.

ABOVE: The statue of Jean-Baptiste de La Quintinie, Louis XIV's gardener who developed the garden for the king.

at the classical design altar of order, clarity, and symmetry, blending house and garden as a cohesive whole into the landscape. Through the implementation of meticulous planting schemes and manipulation of optical illusions, le Notre utilized spacial components to develop sight lines that would lead the eye up toward the sky and out to distant horizons of magnificent vistas. Extensive tree-lined allées, roads, and buildings were established to give focus and open the view to the surrounding countryside, giving a feeling of infinity and beyond.

The second, Jean-Baptiste de La Quintinie, concentrated on growing vegetables and training fruit in espaliered forms, for it was his duty to supply an abundance of fresh food for the king's table. He built Louis's new vegetable garden precisely where he wanted it—on a swamp that was situated near the palace (which required a great movement of earth), making it easy for the king to visit his garden and his gardener every day. It was La Quintinie who became Bunny's hero.

"When the time came to plant my own fruit trees, I made a search for books and instruction on

The Cathedral of Saint Louis, Versailles, in the
background of the basin, which the Mellons restored
at le Potager du Roi.

this special subject." Her first "prize" was a copy of the 1821 *Le Jardin Fruitier* by Louis Claude Noisette (1772–1849). She found the illustrations "inspiring" and admired the "sheer beauty" of the book itself. However, a difficulty in translation led to the discovery of La Quintinie, "the extraordinary seventeenth-century gardener who introduced methods of fruit culture and pruning that are still followed today throughout Europe." The king's vegetable garden, le Potager du Roi, "planned three hundred years ago still exists today, a living witness to the wisdom and theories of La Quintinie, where acres of espalier fruit trees are protected by the Government of France."

ABOVE: Bunny Mellon was taught how to prune these espaliers by the gardeners at le Potager du Roi.

OPPOSITE: Seasonal flowers blossom in front of rows of espaliered fruit in the shadow of the Cathedral of Saint Louis, Versailles.

ABOVE: Artfully pruned fruit trees blossom with the first blush of springtime.

OPPOSITE: An apple tree trained in an espalier form known as a candelabra.

For Bunny Mellon, an ardent self-taught lover of the out-of-doors, gardening and landscaping were one and the same, both a way of "making your own place" and a means of "expressing the visual, emotional aesthetic and useful ways of nature" that are within reach of each of us in our everyday lives. She felt that "the need of each human being is different" and that each person reacts to beauty in their own way. For example, whether we realize it or not, we all notice the efforts of others whether we're strolling down a city street or driving along a country road. Often, we initially forget what we've seen, "until one day something strikes a chord" and we remember and react with a desire to look further or look back. It could be something you passed by on a road-way—an orchard cloaked in wildflowers, a forest thick with evergreens dappled with darting shafts of light, or a single tree that stood alone in a vast empty space. These casual observations should be noted because they can become our "greatest teachers," Bunny believed.

Bunny was a voracious reader, and starting in a small way she began to assemble a collection of books. "Years of curiosity have added botanical and horticultural studies, garden designs, drawings of plants, biographies of naturalists and explorers, accounts of their ships, their journeys, and their discoveries. Everyday books on gardening and related subjects have been collected over the years and now most of the great books have been added" to her collection. It isn't a collection based on a bookseller's recommendation, but each volume was "picked one by one for its unique quality and interest, not as part of a long list of well-known flower books. Time and space did not allow for clutter or random acquisition." She didn't store her books in "dusty darkness" but stashed them under the bed, stacked them on shelves, and dedicated a room in the house so the collection was accessible, because she read them! Soon it became clear that the growing collection would require a new home, and a small library was built on the farm, not far from the garden. Here the collection would be carefully organized "behind simple, pale oak doors, easily opened to the world they tell about."

"These reflections of a lifetime interest are kept in a whitewashed building made of local stone, a gift from my husband Paul. It stands in an open field, wildflowers grow where they will, apple trees are espaliered to the east and west. Inside, the sun casts long, bright shadows across the room onto the white stone walls . . . Two large glass doors create an opening twelve feet square in the long wall, framing an ancient hackberry whose lacy branches are caught up in witches' brooms. Beyond this is a rolling landscape of grass and corn fields, outlined in native trees: dogwoods, willows, maples, and ashes."

ABOVE: A view of the Mellon family farm.

LEFT: The Lower Terrace in Bunny's Oak Spring Garden. A vegetable garden is in the foreground, her Basket House (where she kept baskets) is in the background to the left, and the School House is to the right.

ABOVE: A flower bed of mustard in full bloom glows in golden hues on the Lower Terrace.

LEFT: Bunny enjoyed letting plants roam across the irregular pieces of slate that covered the terraces and pathways.

Herbs were a favorite. "From the beginning of early civilization to the present, herbs have played an extraordinary role. Whether gathered for curing the sick from all walks of life, for cooking or seasoning of foods, or for aromatic and aesthetic purposes, herbs continue to be grown and studied to benefit our basic needs and wants."

And, "as defined by Liberty Hyde Bailey in The Standard Cyclopedia of Horticulture," an herb 'is a plant that dies to the ground each year, or at least that does not become woody. It may be annual, as bean, pigweed; biennial, as mullein, parsnip; perennial, as dictamnus, rhubarb.' As one can clearly see, this type of classification covers a wide spectrum of plants!"

In the summertime, herbs proliferate in the fields around the library and on the terraces, their tender roots taking hold in the bits of earth between the chinks of stone. "The most common ones are the Common Mullein, Dandelion, Plantain, Poke Weed, and Yarrow." Bunny let the herbs grow to seed, and it wasn't uncommon for her to allow the mulleins that had self-planted by the front door to reach their full height, appearing like sentries guarding the gate. Equally so, she prized a single-stem dandelion that found its way into the garden and was alarmed one day to find that a gardener had plucked it out. Lesson learned: nothing was a weed until Mrs. Mellon said it was. "Watching these charming plants grow truly helps to bring our books, drawings, and manuscripts to life by blending the past with the present and future. It is also very interesting to see how many of the old-fashioned remedies that are mentioned in these early books and manuscripts are still in use today."

THE KENNEDY ROSE GARDEN UNFOLDS

Bunny and President Kennedy shared a mutual admiration for America's third president, Thomas Jefferson. While living in the White House, Jefferson had lined windowsills with potted geraniums and kept a running list of vegetables available in the nearby market while making revisions to the building itself. John Kennedy wasn't lining any windowsills with plants, but he was concocting a project that would require a transformation of the old Rose Garden, which filled the space between the White House residence and the West Wing. This plot was first gardened by First Lady Edith Roosevelt. It was a space that had opened up after a sprawl of greenhouses had been demolished, creating way for her husband Teddy's new office building, the West Wing. A couple of administrations later, the same outdoor space was redesigned by First Lady Ellen Wilson, who filled it with roses and renamed it accordingly. From then on, other than the weekly mowing and trimming, Ellen's garden was largely ignored for the next forty years by successive presidents Harding, Coolidge, Hoover, Roosevelt, Truman, and Eisenhower.

Kennedy's plan covered new ground. He wanted to stretch the proverbial walls of the Oval Office into the garden, creating a green theater—

an outdoor stage—where he would showcase his ideas and parade his triumphant New Frontier policies before the American people on a worldwide scale. His "precise and clear" request for a new garden became for Bunny Mellon a labor of love. And for Kennedy? Well, over time the garden became known as President Kennedy's Rose Garden, and through the advent of television sealed his place in political history as up-and-coming television networks beamed their nightly newscasts into America's living rooms, replete with staged images of the president at work in the lushly planted garden.

It was Bunny Mellon who had quietly made it all happen. Her process seemed doable; her standards of garden design thoughtful, exacting, and straight to the point. Even President Kennedy seemed to enjoy watching the project unfold and appreciated how she got things done. One can only imagine how the keenly observant Kennedy had probably wished his capable friend would also agree to take a seat at the Cabinet table, too.

Kennedy was in a hurry to begin, and at his request, Bunny visited the Rose Garden site to analyze the existing space and evaluate the setting. From where she sat that first day under Andrew Jackson's overgrown magnolia trees studying the area all around, she remembered thinking, "This end of the White House looked like a pale man staring into space." The coat of white paint

In the northern flower bed of the Rose Garden
at the White House, 'Katherine' crabapples
planted in repeating diamonds of santolina are
surrounded by flowers in season.

that Teddy Roosevelt had splashed over the old sandstone walls created a harsh, sterile effect. Being solution oriented, Bunny's thoughts turned toward remedies and the need to "soften all that white." Likewise, she had to decide on a boundary, because she always designed a "landscape with fixed horizons, whether it be mountains or a stone wall." And if there wasn't a set boundary, then she would have to create one. The Rose Garden is hemmed in on three sides by the West Wing, the connecting colonnade, and the White House. The remaining side opens to the south lawn with the Washington Monument and the Jefferson Memorial in the sight line.

Bunny's next step was to develop a plan that, of course, included the president's wish list and remained true to the historical site itself. It was a short list that included a lawn area large enough for the president to host up to a thousand people for receptions, awards of merit ceremonies, and press conferences. He wanted colorful flowers in season and a set of new steps that would function more as a platform than a set of steps. And, finally, he wanted a garden that "would return to the peace and silence of a private garden" when all those people had left.

Landscape design, "like all design, is personal. It is the expression of the people involved." The landscape "must put together things of nature that correspond to the person as well as to the place and environment. It must inspire, calm, and please," and, in this case, contribute to the "president's well-being." This involved creating "an overall outline," what she called "the 'bone structure.' It was the most important element," she wrote in her article "President Kennedy's Garden" for the White House Historical Association's journal *White House History*. "You begin with the skeleton sketch, a general pleasing outline, or form, and proceed from there. Within this structure, you can make subdivisions as you choose, more complicated or more detailed than the general form." She noted the space, took measurements, observed the movement of the sun, where the light shined in the day and where the shadows fell at dusk. She calculated potential difficulties, anticipated solutions, gathered her team, and—following her own set of garden design standards—began.

Mrs. Mellon hired Irvin Williams away from the National Park Service and Everett Hicks from the Davey Tree Company. Local D.C. landscape architect Perry Wheeler rounded out the Mellon team. All three men were experts in their fields. Friendships among Bunny and these men, forged in the garden, lasted several lifetimes.

OPPOSITE: Bunny Mellon with her arborist, Everett Hicks, planting a *Magnolia x soulangeana* in the Rose Garden at the White House.

Her White House garden design hinged on four *Magnolia x soulangeana* (saucer magnolia) that she, Williams, and Wheeler sourced from East and West Potomac Parks in Washington, D.C. Facing abject rejection from the National Park Service, which insisted the trees would not fit in the garden space, Wheeler quietly insisted they would. Williams quietly had the trees moved to a nearby holding area, and when planting day came, Hicks quietly planted them in their allotted corners while President Kennedy carried on with his work in the Oval Office. The magic of the trees in the garden was due in part to Hicks's skillful pruning. "He had the touch," Williams said. Standing on top of a ladder on top of a flatbed cart, Hicks trimmed the trees, sculpting the tips into "patterns that edged the sky." The gently rolling tree canopy was a distinguishing feature at all of the Mellon estates.

OPPOSITE: One of four *Magnolia x soulangeana* planted in the Rose Garden, this one is directly outside the Oval Office. The First Division Monument, which honors the soldiers who fought in World War I, can be seen in the background.

ABOVE: A view across the southern border of the Rose Garden to the south grounds of the White House during the Kennedy presidency.

BUNNY'S GARDEN STANDARDS

*"To become a good gardener, you have to
spend time every day in the garden."*

Bunny's garden standards are a result of her daily discipline of spending time in her gardens, pushing through the ups and downs, celebrating the successes and coping with the failures—all of which equal the sum total of any gardener's experience, or anyone learning a new trade, for that matter. While Bunny considered all of her standards to be of the utmost importance, time spent in the garden was probably her number-one unspoken rule. If you don't show up, then what's the point?

One day, a friend, Babe Paley, came to her Oak Spring farm to learn about gardening and landscape design. Babe and her husband, William Paley, were in the throes of building a new estate on Long Island, and she looked to Bunny for advice. After a couple of days spent at the farm, Bunny let Babe in on this little secret: *To become a good gardener, you have to spend time every day in the garden*—which meant she'd have to curtail her social life. This was an incomprehensible thought, a foreign concept, to a woman who topped the New York City social register. Babe fled home to New York and sent her gardener back to Oak Spring instead.

The pages of the garden book that Bunny drafted in her journals were probably intended for friends like Babe. "It would be short," she said, most likely hoping it would actually be read. "A few suggestions that would encourage beginners and a few warnings not to

ABOVE: The road that Bunny designed to pass through the flower-laden arbor between the garden and library to reach the east side of the farm.

OPPOSITE: Shadows and light paint a lattice design on the path below the arbor that connects the garden with the Formal Greenhouse.

overdo. No matter how you start, you will change your ideas with experience. If you are sincerely interested in the subject, experience will carry you along. Sometimes with disappointments, but they too sharpen and further your knowledge as you search for a replacement or another approach."

Even after President Kennedy's death, Bunny carried on and continued to dig in the Rose Garden, prune the trees, pull weeds, and give advice as the White House gardeners, successive presidents, and first ladies alike continued to reach out to her. And now, almost sixty years later,

the garden speaks for itself. It has stood the test of time, remaining faithful to Bunny's original plan, which was crafted on the strength of her garden standards.

The standards that she adhered to and her thoughts on these standards—the importance of making a garden plan, measuring, the considerations of atmosphere, horizons, sight lines, light, space, and shadows—were recorded throughout her journal writings.

"Before planning a garden, find out how the garden or space to be landscaped will be used."

Ask questions that are fundamental to the site. Where is the garden located? Where is the horizon? What are the sight lines and where are the boundaries? Is there a water supply? What is the climate? What is the soil composition and what amendments are necessary? What does the existing space allow for? "What is natural and in harmony with the existing building and country-side?" "Where does the wind come from that is harsh in winter? In summer, where does the house cast shadows?" "What will the upkeep require?" What exists—a garage, a large tree? And what do you want? What are you most interested in? There is no use in "designing a garden that will lose its shape and design in a few years."

OPPOSITE: The wishing well on the Lower Terrace near a vegetable patch filled with greens ready for harvest. The Basket House and School House are in the background.

ABOVE: A view of the Lower Terrace in the Oak Spring Garden facing northeast. Flourishing cordons line the garden paths.

RIGHT: Spring, a favorite time in the garden, when the deep red of the tulips subtly enhances the beauty of the Square Garden at Oak Spring.

OPPOSITE: The Upper Terrace and Square Garden of the Oak Spring Garden.

ABOVE: The garden at Cape Cod was located a short distance from the house and enclosed by a tall hedge to buffer it from the ocean winds. A sundial punctuates the point where two garden paths crisscross. The drying shed is to the left and the greenhouse to the right.

ABOVE: The Cape Cod garden in spring is being prepared for summer's floral show. In the background is the Drying Shed, where flowers were hung from the rafters for drying.

OPPOSITE: The Cape Cod garden in full bloom at the height of summer. Whimsical weather vanes crowned the peaks of many of Bunny's buildings.

PLANNING AND MEASURING FOR YOUR GARDEN

"Gardens have been written about throughout the ages. But, like many beautiful things, one thinks they will never change—never cease to be what they are. Never die. Unfortunately, they follow the cycle of all living things—never remaining the same. It is well then to take notes that will help to remind those in later years of all they possessed—so that they may imagine, dream and perhaps recall a part of what has been."

As you begin to design your garden, write down your thoughts, interests, and vision for the garden along with what you would like to have in your garden. Organize your ideas, take notes, and plan. "Don't buy things at random. Like bad habits in other ways, one can start bad garden habits."

Bunny discussed how to plan a garden in her article "The Garden Plan," Excerpts follow on pages 54, 55 and 60:

OPPOSITE: The west side of the Upper Terrace in the Oak Spring Garden. In this photograph, Bunny has used a black marker to circle a plant that requires further attention.

ABOVE: A neat and tidy vegetable plot by one of seven barns at Rokeby Stables, where Paul Mellon raised horses for fox hunting and flat racing.

A garden should be planned as a whole, she advised.

"You may never complete your plan for twenty years, but if every bit of effort you put in is working toward the completion of a plan as a whole, you save both time and money. If someday you should wake up and decide you must have a vegetable garden, and with this inspiration, rush out and dig any old spot without thought to the future, and then, the next year you feel inspired to build a garden pool, the chances are the very place you put your vegetable garden will be the most advantageous spot for the garden pool. So that year spent in getting the soil in condition for the vegetables will be wasted as you dig it up to make the pool. However, with your big eraser, these things can be jiggled around like a Chinese puzzle."

STEP 1: Make a list of "all your problems, such as a garage or laundry yard you want to hide, an ugly pump or a muddy walk that needs repair."

STEP 2: "Make a second list of all the things you eventually hope to have, as cold frames, tool house, vegetable garden, etc."

STEP 3: "Measure the actual length of your house, garden, paths, and whatever you want to know, and write these down on paper."

"After you have all your necessary measurements, come in, put up your table by a nice fire and settle down."

STEP 4: On the graph paper, use your measurements and "draw the outline of all existing buildings, and important trees, remembering to draw in the area that is shaded by these trees. Also mark the points of the compass, so as to be sure where the sun will be."

STEP 5: "Next come the colored pencils." "Make improvements or changes with an ordinary pencil . . . When you are sure of a new change it can be drawn in red."

OPPOSITE: The grassy center path leading up to the greenhouse in the Cape Cod garden. A central workroom for the gardeners was flanked by two Lord and Burnham greenhouses.

RIGHT: Bunny Mellon was a hands-on gardener who spent time with her hired gardeners and builders working in the garden or reviewing plans—whatever the day required. She is pictured here, wearing her trademark garden hat, at her house on Nantucket.

At the Nantucket property, there was a small raised garden bed enclosed with wood fencing that was brushed in streaks with Bunny's own paint formula to give a head start to the weathering process.

ABOVE, LEFT: A working greenhouse built with slats was located near the vegetable garden in Antigua.

ABOVE, RIGHT: A view of the Antigua compound called King's Leap.

LEFT: The gardens were covered with lattice structures called "hats" to screen the tender plants from the strong heat of the midday sun.

OPPOSITE: King's Leap, the Mellon Antigua compound, is located on a bluff high above Half Moon Bay. A shaded pool is seen in the foreground.

ABOVE: Looking across the property to Half Moon Bay and the horizon. **BELOW, LEFT:** Bunny Mellon ready for a day in the sunshine. **BELOW, RIGHT:** Paul Mellon comfortably dressed in swim shorts.

Whether making a new garden or improving an existing one, the garden planner must first gather the necessary supplies: graph paper, "a ruler, a long measuring tape, some colored pencils, and a good eraser." On a practical note, always measure your space. It simplifies things and prevents mistakes. Bunny worked alongside her gardeners as they planted and encouraged them to "train your eye to measure. If you learn what three feet is in your mind's eye, then you can imagine one foot—three feet—or six—or nine." Then, once you've measured, make a little sketch so that planting will not be a "hit and miss game." "There are rules." Follow them. Be respectful of how much space each plant requires. Don't overplant.

"One of the most important things to remember, if you are planning a garden, is to keep your eyes open. Driving along a road, no matter how often you have traveled it before, you may get an idea. Either what to do or what not to do. I don't mean ever to copy someone else's idea, for it would not give you the same pleasure as if you had thought it out for yourself. But change it around. For instance, I saw a small dilapidated barn about twenty feet high with a shed on one side. Its lines were good, and I thought what an attractive garage that would make if you used the same dimensions and design, using the loft as a workshop and the shed off one side, with its corn crib as a shelter for tools, and a place to dry herbs and such things."

Oak Spring, the Mellon family home situated in
the foothills of the Blue Ridge mountains, has
the feeling of a French hamlet. It is comprised
of numerous connected outbuildings named the
Guest House, Basket House, Honey House, and
School House.

Bunny created country roads that blended seamlessly
with nature so that nothing would be noticed or
distracting to the eye. Her philosophy of blending
into nature is evident here.

ATMOSPHERE

"Every garden has its own way of being."

"Each garden has its own atmosphere. Apart from the differences of location, soil, climate, etc., many of the differences come from the personal ideas of those involved—how they see it, their way of life and needs."

Atmosphere can be created through choice of plants.

• Select native plant material, consider the fashion in plants—is there a heavy or a light feeling?

• There must always be space between small or large leaves.

• Consider the color of the bark in winter, trees and shrubs against large and tall buildings.

ABOVE: A pink flowering quince clings to the corner wall of Mellon gardener J. D. Tutwiler's office, which was located near the Oak Spring Garden.

OPPOSITE: Brick pathways laid in herringbone and basket-weave patterns crisscross the Oak Spring Garden. Tall wooden gates are closed at dusk and opened in the morning.

OPPOSITE, ABOVE LEFT: Bunny enjoyed listening to the soft sounds of water trickling through the garden. The lip of this rustic waterfall is a flat rock that looks like a turtle shell. It was found by stone mason Tommy Reed in a village near Oak Spring. OPPOSITE, ABOVE RIGHT: The courtyard entry of the main house at Oak Spring. Sprigs of common thyme and fleabane daisies ramble about, while Kingsville Boxwoods soften the sharp edges of the locally quarried slate. OPPOSITE, BELOW: A slice of the Basket House pool fronts a sheltered niche. Bunny dipped her baskets in the pool to refresh and clean them.

ABOVE: A wall of dry stacked stone forms a boundary line. LEFT: The view east across the Square Garden and the Upper Terrace. The Honey House can be seen in the background. It was used as a garden shed, not to store honey.

OPPOSITE: Inside the Formal Greenhouse, which was her winter garden.

ABOVE: The Formal Greenhouse, where Bunny wintered her citrus and little herb trees.

LEFT: Bunny posing in front of her first greenhouse at the Lambert family house, Carter Hall, in Millwood, Virginia.

A vision of "utmost simplicity" is an 1800s New England house with the atmosphere of seventeenth-century style, which Bunny had moved to the Mellon Cape Cod compound "by the sea," with air, salt, fog, a distant horizon line, and the sounds of gulls and geese streaking through the sky—"and silence." "Stark at its foundation," for this particular landscape one must consider the wind and the elements, use native plants (wild poppies, grapes, blackberries, roses, beach plums, and bayberry), and "plant as the wind blows." A vegetable garden and orchard must be planted as a thing apart and should be surrounded by a hedge of trees or shrubs pruned to a "low height as a buttress against the wind."

OPPOSITE: The fruit orchard in the garden at Cape Cod.

ABOVE, LEFT: At Cape Cod, a regular visitor perches daily on this neat hand-wrapped teepee.

ABOVE, RIGHT: Walls are cloaked in roses in summertime.

ABOVE: The view of Seapuit River from Bunny's bedroom window at Cape Cod. The strip of land to the left is a barrier island called Dead Neck Island. It buffers the narrow river from the choppy waves of Nantucket Sound. Bunny used the path in the foreground to reach the beach where she enjoyed morning swims.

OPPOSITE, ABOVE: Irregular pieces of slate placed like stepping stones across the lawn border of the Crescent Garden, located directly above the river. Nantucket Sound is in the distance.

OPPOSITE, BELOW: A wooden goose, one of two geese that flank the walkway leading to the beach.

Views of the Nantucket property. **OPPOSITE, ABOVE LEFT:** Waves of the Atlantic Ocean crash on the shore below Bunny's house in Nantucket. **OPPOSITE, ABOVE RIGHT:** Bunny's style was to mix flower varieties in her beds. **OPPOSITE, BELOW LEFT:** The Nantucket house was painted yellow and protected by surrounding walls. **OPPOSITE, BELOW RIGHT:** Blue-eyed grass cloaks the fields of the Nantucket property in summertime.

ABOVE: Raised beds in the enclosed Nantucket garden.

ABOVE: A view of English Harbour in Antigua.

OPPOSITE, ABOVE: In Antigua a pool is enclosed with a lattice treillage. Obelisk designed by Paul Leonard.

OPPOSITE, BELOW LEFT: A barefoot Bunny, always happiest with pruning shears in hand.

OPPOSITE, BELOW RIGHT: Pruning brings shape and a tidy appearance to a courtyard tree.

ABOVE: Two white benches were placed on opposite sides of the Cape Cod vegetable garden.

OPPOSITE: A terrace outside Bunny's Sunday kitchen at Oak Spring.

ABOVE, LEFT: Garden terrace at Bunny and Paul Mellon's New York City townhouse.

ABOVE, RIGHT: The terrace at the Mellons' Paris apartment is not dissimilar to their terrace in New York.

BELOW: Sheltering in place in the Dune House garden surrounded by herbs and flowers of the season.

OPPOSITE, ABOVE: The townhouse garden in New York City. Four identical Italian obelisks punctuated the corners of the center bed, planted with ivy and boxwood.

OPPOSITE, BELOW: A still life scene on the terrace at the New York City townhouse.

LIGHT AND SHADOW

"Light especially has a great influence on the mood. I will write about this one day."

"Light is one of the most important things to consider." Plants need light for food production, and different plants need different degrees of light. In garden design, one "must anticipate all available sources of light."

Light changes throughout the day and across the seasons—shifting from the sharp light of a sunny morning and afternoon, to the softening light of the evening as it blends into the golden glow of sunset, to gray days when the atmosphere is full of mystery and overcast.

LEFT: Purple alliums bending into the light on the pathway beneath the Oak Spring arbor.

ABOVE: Dappled light shines through a flower border in the Oak Spring Garden.

OPPOSITE, ABOVE: A view of the pool to the west of the arbor.

OPPOSITE, BELOW: Bunny casting a long shadow over the garden at her beloved Oak Spring.

"Different parts of any country have their own light," and where the sun falls differs through the year. There is light by the sea, in the mountains, down in the valleys, and in the desert. White light is the most difficult type of light, as it gives a gray, lifeless light. In consideration of the light, one must also consider the darkness—especially where the shadows fall.

"Shadows are a great part of a garden." They give life and "can be anticipated before planting" by finding "the path of the sun." Shadows can be "controlled by pruning" as well as by the shapes and forms of the plant material selected. Trees with small leaves that bend in the breeze and move easily—like locust, aspen, and Russian olive—cast shadows that move and sometimes appear to "dance on the ground." "Espaliered trees that are planted close to a wall cast shadows of different values and atmosphere."

ABOVE: Plants were allowed to roam and hug the edges of this pathway between the Square Garden and the Upper Terrace.

RIGHT: Puppy dog Patrick sitting in a shady doorway beside a tree laden with lemons.

OPPOSITE: Close-up of an espaliered fruit tree. Bunny enjoyed watching the changing light against the whitewashed wall throughout the day. There was always something new to see.

"Take care to select light-colored foliage and gray trees," Bunny cautioned. The colors of the bark and the way the leaves flutter in the breeze can produce light. Trees to consider include locust, olives, apples, and aspen. Dark trees can be used as accents. Light can be bounced off of walls to create shadows and add atmosphere to a setting.

BELOW: A tree-shaded terrace in Antigua with a view of the house.

OPPOSITE, ABOVE: Two courtyard gates are splashed in Bunny's favorite color—blue.

OPPOSITE, BELOW: The King's Leap entryway balcony is reflected in the illuminated courtyard pool below.

SPACE

"When I see any landscaped area for the first time, I automatically look for how much space has been allowed to remain. That means how much sky, how much air."

"When I think of gardens—of planting and growing plants—one of the first thoughts is of space—small or large," because a garden is all the space—the landscape that is yours to put together. "You must always think of landscaping from mountain to mountain—or the horizon line. What you put in between makes the dimensions."

This principle can also be used in small spaces by working with a boundary line. A planted hedge or wall that is formed in a straight line to create a boundary line, with an open sky above, will bring in the distance and whatever is there—mountains, another building, or the horizon. This will be "your beginning" and the sky will be "your biggest plus."

OPPOSITE: The orchard at Oak Spring spreads
across the hillside.

ABOVE: The north side of the Oak Spring Garden
Library with a view of the Blue Ridge Mountains in
the distance.

ABOVE: This pristine white cottage established a beginning point—a boundary line—at the Nantucket property. The repetitive roofline leads the eye into the distance and the sky above. Bunny considered the sky to be the designer's "biggest asset."

OPPOSITE, ABOVE: A view of the crescent garden above Seapuit River at the Mellon house on Cape Cod.

OPPOSITE, BELOW: Arborist Bobby Childs, affectionately known as "the treeman," was thought to have spent more time in the treetops than on the ground.

"Space is more than a land-locked boundary line. Space is also looking up." And this is precisely why modern buildings like the East Wing at the National Gallery of Art, magnificently designed by I. M. Pei, are so exciting. They frame space, "giving it dimension after dimension," making you aware of the sky space.

Then there is the sea. "We live by the sea. So the sea as far as your eye can reach is part of the small piece of land you own. What you do with this land takes in the sea—or not."

Regardless of size, you must imagine a garden with forms. This includes the size of trees and the way that they are pruned. "A well-pruned garden can catch and support the snow or ice, giving for a brief moment a garden of enchantment" and a "surprise in the garden," as well.

"Looking at primitive drawings of farms and gardens, we are fascinated by their charm. It is the emptiness and obvious places where things can be planted that attracts us. But if over-planted, the charm is gone. So, no matter where you start, do not overplant. And do not be in a hurry. Each thing relates to the next."

ABOVE: An aerial view of Oak Spring facing south.

OPPOSITE: A Mount Vernon–style garden shed abuts the serpentine wall that Bunny designed for the Brick House garden at Oak Spring.

ABOVE: Hubert de Givenchy's country garden at
Château du Jonchet.

OPPOSITE: Whirling beds of boxwood aligned with
fruit trees in perfect symmetry.

Renovating a Garden

"If you are renovating an old garden, some decisions will have been made for you; but if you are starting from scratch, there are important questions you must ask yourself: Where am I going to plant? This is important, for it will answer the questions of light and shade, soil, sun, drainage, water supply, and so on.

"The second question is 'what do I want in a design?' What do you want to grow and what feeling are you trying to achieve? Is it to be a garden for flowers, herbs, fruit, enclosures, boundary lines, trees, a courtyard, terraces, etc.? It could be for all or just one of these."

"The choice of materials is important depending on the architecture of the building you are working with. In France, for instance, I was doing a garden at a château. The roof lines were the most pure. The strength of the forest through which an allée had been cut radiating into the distance needed no more than what the owner did—clear up and eliminate dead trees and branches."

Hubert de Givenchy shared a story about gardening with Bunny. "One day she said, 'Hubert, you must cut down this forest.'" They had been collaborating on the restoration of Louis XIV's le Potager du Roi at the Palace of Versailles and, upon its completion, had turned their thoughts and imaginations toward Givenchy's landscape and the making of a potager at his Manoir du Jonchet. "It is important to let the light in," she

BELOW: A thicket of yellow lilies creates a focal point at Le Jonchet.

OPPOSITE: Hedges are used to effect in a formal landscape design at Le Jonchet.

LEFT: Bands of tulips seemingly rejoice beneath a stunning sky.

BELOW AND OPPOSITE: Views of the Butterfly Parterre located on the Middle Terrace in the Oak Spring Garden. Look closely and you will see the gentle curving outline of a butterfly "drawn" with brick pavers.

explained to him. When asked if he had heeded her advice, he exclaimed, "No! It was a forest of trees!" and added, "It was a good thing, too, because she called a few days later and said 'she'd changed her mind!' She told me, 'Hubert, I have changed my mind about the forest and decided that you shouldn't have cut it down.'

"Incredible!" he exclaimed, his face lit up with emotion. "Imagine what it would have cost me to replant all of those trees! I told her, 'Bunny, we must go slowly!'"

While helping her friend redesign portions of his estate landscape in France, Bunny designed something similar to what she had in her Oak Spring Garden, where symmetrical imprints of two butterfly images are outlined in bricks on one of the parterres. In early spring, the butterfly beds are filled with herbs and annuals, and in summer the garden comes alive with the dancing and fluttering of these delicate creatures. In winter, after the plants have been cut back, the outlines of the butterfly images create a sweet memory of summer.

Bunny created a similar design in France at Givenchy's Manoir du Jonchet, where a hundred-year-old oak tree grew near the château. She wrote, "We marked the exact area where it cast its summer shadow, it's 'great shadow,' and planted it with hundreds of lapis-blue Scillas." "This surprise of lapis blue blooming in the grass each spring lasted only two weeks each year and had a magical quality. And the bulbs multiplied, becoming bluer each year. When the flowers bloom, their blueness is like a memory of that great shadow." And, she continued, "a house of this structure, period, and noblesse cannot have flowered borders in evidence."

It is better that flowers like narcissus, violets, and other wood-like plants "appear in large drifts under the trees."

OPPOSITE: Bunny enjoying the hillside planted with her favorite blue Scilla. She and Givenchy planted the shadow of a tree with Scilla at Jonchet to create "a memory of summer."

ABOVE: The farmlands with the distant view of Oak Spring in the background.

BELOW: Sweeps of Scilla cover a hillside at Oak Spring.

ABOVE: A field of wildflowers that was cultivated in the Cape Cod landscape.

OPPOSITE, ABOVE: Everyday life in the garden at Cape Cod. Sprays of water from a garden hose shower a sculptured sundial.

OPPOSITE, BELOW: The Cape Cod house was reached at the end of a lane that curves through a stand of pruned trees.

INSIGHTS ON INSECTS

Lest we imagine that Bunny Mellon's gardens were somehow free of the common pests that invade flower and vegetable gardens, here are excerpts from a gardening article she published in 1938 in the *Clarke Courier* titled "Chewing and Sucking Bugs." It was a dissertation on the infestation of green aphids that covered her "climbing roses, English ivy, willows, and countless other things" so that she couldn't move "without a sprayer" in hand. "Everywhere I look my eyes light on masses of green aphids."

"These horrible pests are among the many insects known as sucking insects. They do not chew but destroy by sucking the juices from them. To me they are more difficult to control as their damage is well underway by the time I have discovered it. With the green aphids, it is easy, as you can see them, but in the case of Red Spider, a whole bush may become affected before you know it. I guess maybe I am lazy or stupid, but I have yet to catch this pest before he has done his worst.

"Speaking of Red Spider, the very best cure for him is to give him a case of pneumonia. He catches it easily and by a thorough sprinkling of cold water repeatedly, is soon done away with. Mealy bugs, scales, and trips all belong to this class of pest, and their work is detected when leaving; [the leaves] curl under, become misshapen, or turn yellow. And, when the bark on shrubs such as lilacs get a rough, whitish cover. They are a particularly choosy high-hat type of pest. Never would they make a meal of potatoes or some ordinary annual when they can get hold of your boxwood, French lilac, or Jacotte rose. To combat them, one must choke them. They breathe through their pores in their body, and such things as nicotine spray, lime sulphur, oil sprays, and soap solutions must be used.

"The other type of pest is known as the chewing insect, or as I mentally think of him, the one with scissors. He cuts things off at the ground, cuts patterns in leaves, cuts leaves off entirely, and in general acts like anyone with a pair of scissors and nothing to do. Even now, as I am writing, I know that my Delphinium are being devoured by a white, squirmy cutworm, all because I did not make collars and put around them. Collars are strips of tin about two inches wide, 15 inches long that I encircle the plant with and stick in the ground about an inch deep. It is a better way to get rid of cutworms than the usual poison bait, which is so easily picked up by birds."

On Friday, June 3, 1938, her article "The Grand Hotel for Bugs" in the *Clarke Courier* led with, "The other day while wandering around the garden inspecting the damage of the storm, I noticed that my 'Snow in Summer' was beginning to crowd out everything around it. In trying to thin it out, to my horror I found the ground under it covered with every imaginable bug including snails, cutworms, and termites. All I could think of was that I had come unaware upon 'The Grand Hotel for Bugs.' They had been nicely protected during the bad weather and were no doubt waiting for their chance to take on my garden."

Obeying her first inclination to remove the plant and "catch every occupant"—which she did—she soon realized a part of the plant could have been saved and regretted the hasty action. "So," she cautioned, "do not follow my method. However, I strongly advise, if you own any plant which sprawls over the ground, that you inspect it immediately as you, too, may be running such a hostelry without knowing it. This all sounds like a lot of nonsense, but all my many months of work would be in vain had these various bugs gone to work."

A cooling green-and-white color palette permeates this woodland scene.

THE IMPORTANCE
OF TREES

"Pruning large trees gives a feeling of
being part of the universe."

Trees were Bunny's first love and often the beginning of a garden plan. "Learn your trees, shrubs, plants like an artist's palette." Memorize tree names. Bunny used trees as sculpture and as the "bones of her gardens." Trees anchor the garden plan, add atmosphere, and cast their blessed shade, which is so precious on hot summer days. They become "focal points from which flower, vegetable, and herb beds evolve."

"Part of creating is understanding that there is always more to do; nothing is ever completely finished," Bunny told the *New York Times* feature writer Paula Deitz for a June 3, 1982, article titled "The Private World of a Great Gardener" where Paula described "one of Rachel Lambert Mellon's most elaborate designs . . . an artfully pleached arbor of crabapple trees" that connects the garden to the greenhouse.

For Bunny Mellon, trees were the bones of the garden. She placed them in lines, in groups, and singly.

"An allée is a lush and inviting walkway lined with trees," stated Mellon family friends Michael Valentine Bartlett and Rose Love Bartlett in their book *The Bartlett Book of Garden Elements: A Practical Compendium of Inspired Designs for the Working Gardener* (David R. Godine, Publisher, Boston, MA, 2014). "Trees arranged symmetrically

LEFT: Stands of deciduous trees color the Oak Spring landscape in the fall.

ABOVE: A pea-gravel pathway crosses the garden, leading to a mighty oak, a symbol of power and strength.

OPPOSITE, ABOVE: Low, dry-stacked walls built of locally quarried stone create boundaries and bring order to the Oak Spring farmlands.

OPPOSITE, BELOW: A stand of sculptured trees adorns a distant view of the Blue Ridge Mountains.

ABOVE: The yearly harvest brought an abundance of apples. The vintage varieties were used in the kitchens at Oak Spring and Cape Cod. Bunny gave some of the apples as personal gifts in peck baskets that were made at a local basket company and also shared the fruit with nearby schools and local nonprofits.

in lines have been incorporated into gardens throughout the ages as a way to connect and feature outbuildings, create focal points, frame garden vistas, and provide shade and shelter." André le Notre used allées to "structure the vast open spaces and provide direction, definition, and welcome shade," the Bartletts agreed. On the other hand, the Bartlett's wrote, "An arbor can be defined as either a leafy, shady niche formed by tree branches or shrubs, or a latticework bower intertwined with climbing vines and flowers."

OPPOSITE: Bunny planted an abundance of Hardy Orange trees in the Oak Spring gardens because the thorny branches provided shelter for the birds and bore pretty ornamental fruit in season.

ABOVE: Sweeps of golden flowering mustard fill the Lower Terrace in the Oak Spring Garden.

At the Oak Spring Garden in Virginia, Bunny designed a 127-foot walkway that became a latticework bower. It was created to connect the Lord and Burnham greenhouse, her winter garden, to the center path in the Formal Garden. Her arborist, Everett Hicks, who was of the rock star variety in the arborist world, built a steel structure support over the walkway and trained 'Mary Potter' crabapples to follow the length and curve of the structure in a crisscross pattern that formed a lattice design. Today it is a leafy green bower that flowers in springtime and bears red berries in the fall. It was just one of Mr. Hicks' arboreal feats. He traveled to all the Mellon properties instructing the on-site gardeners in all methods of pruning.

'Mary Potter' crabapples are trained over a steel frame, creating an arbor of seasonal delight. The trees were pruned twice a year to allow the air to move through the branches and maintain the shifting lattice design on the pathway below. The crabapples hold their slow-ripening crimson berries throughout the fall. This arbor connects the Formal Garden to the Formal Greenhouse at Oak Spring.

OPPOSITE: The finial on this rooftop is a bouquet of lead flowers arranged in a low, footed urn. Created by French jewelry designer Jean Schlumberger, this magnificent masterpiece blesses the peak of the Formal Greenhouse roof at Oak Spring. Inspired by the Dutch Masters art of floral design, Bunny's bouquet is akin to a still life painting and depicts an array of flowers in phases of bloom throughout the season, from the tiniest of buds to wilting flower heads spent with age.

ABOVE: The entrance to the Formal Greenhouse is festooned with the 'Mary Potter' crabapples and tubs of potted trees.

RIGHT: Clad in her favored cloche-styled garden hat and walk-about espadrilles, Bunny basks in the fruits of her labor beneath the arbor with a friend who appears to have arrived from another century.

OPPOSITE, ABOVE: Ornamental benches strategically placed in shady niches provide respite. Bunny walked the gardens and grounds in all kinds of weather, and she particularly enjoyed feeling the windy gusts and hearing the crash of thunder as lightning crackled in the sky during a summer thunderstorm.

OPPOSITE, BELOW: Down the hill on the east side of the Oak Spring house is a small stone Spring House, where cool water from a natural spring flows into a concrete basin about ten inches deep. The overflow runs through a trough outside the house for about 75 yards, making a creek bed, and then flows into Eliza's Pond.

ABOVE: An artfully pruned tree is a thing of beauty in winter, before the first flush of springtime growth.

OPPOSITE: Variations of shadow and light embellish the view across the farmlands toward the horizons.

ABOVE: Spring bursting forth in all her glory at Oak Spring.

LEFT: A stone trough where water flows from the Middle Terrace into a small pool on the Lower Terrace in Bunny's Oak Spring Garden.

ABOVE: In Nantucket, Bunny got creative and supplanted the real trees that could not survive the harsh easterly exposure with wooden trees. She patterned the designs of the wooden trees after the hawthorn, which provided shelter for the birds and was the name of one of the authors from which her grandfather had read to her as a child.

LEFT: Seeking imperfect perfection, Bunny adjusts a branch on one of her wooden trees.

OPPOSITE: A wooden fence white-washed with Bunny's own aging formula protects a small enclosed garden in Nantucket.

Trees in the landscape presented a challenge at Bunny's Nantucket house. Built on a west-facing bluff above the Atlantic Ocean, the windswept conditions and salty air made it virtually impossible for the trees to survive. Bunny supervised repeated plantings of the hawthorn, hoping to blend atmosphere into the landscape—but the trees didn't survive the heavy salty winds that blew from the Atlantic. Finally, after so much failure, she cleverly adapted one of her garden standards: wooden trees. These are fake trees, 2 x 4s hammered together to represent the size and shape of one of her preferred trees, the hawthorn. Typically, before a final planting, a wooden tree would be staked in place and she would observe the "tree" through the seasons, being especially interested in where the shadows fell. As a last resort, she had the wooden trees staked around the property and it worked! They survived, Bunny had her beloved trees, and they were maintenance free!

PRUNE, PRUNE, PRUNE

Pruned trees that are "sheared at the top have a lovely form and do not get spindly. Trees can be "used as an allée" or for an "orchard planting," as "done by my father at his house in Princeton."

ABOVE: Arborist Bobby Childs, atop a tree on Cape Cod, shirked Bunny's request for everyone to wear a hat at all times. She also made sure the gardeners took breaks and that there was plenty of drinking water available. The Mellons took generous care of their arborists.

LEFT AND OPPOSITE: On most days, there was usually an arborist armed with a long pruning hook perched high in a tree, pruning stray branches to bring light, air, and good health to the trees.

OPPOSITE: A walkway fringed with a cordon of apples and underplanted in a cool palette of flowers that were encouraged to roam freely across the borders and walkways.

ABOVE: Springtime enchantment on the Lower Terrace at Oak Spring.

BELOW: Reminiscent of the gardens in the story *Alice in Wonderland*, Bunny clipped the holly trees into tiers at Oak Spring and in the Jacqueline Kennedy Garden at the White House.

TREES IN ALL SEASONS

Consider trees for their shape, size, and color
throughout the seasons.

ABOVE: An orchard of dormant apple trees in all their gnarled glory dot the landscape of Bunny's library at Oak Spring.

OPPOSITE, ABOVE: Shadows lengthen and the light is subdued as autumn casts its warm golden glow across Oak Spring. To the left is the greenhouse rooftop and to the right is the cluster of shingled buildings known as Oak Spring.

OPPOSITE, BELOW LEFT: Bunny learned the fine art of manipulating trees into shapes called espalier while working with the gardeners at le Potager du Roi in Versailles, France.

OPPOSITE, BELOW RIGHT: A scene of winter serenity. The stark beauty of a tree in the landscape becomes sculpture.

KNOW YOUR TREES INTIMATELY

"Know the forms of trees intimately," and their patterns that are always "edging the sky."

POSITIONING TREES

"Putting trees at a distance and allowing space in between tends to hide the neighbor's house," Bunny wrote. She cautioned not to plant too many trees near the house. "So many houses are hidden by arborvitae. Keep the house free—no base planting."

OPPOSITE: Varieties of stately oak trees dot the Oak Spring property.

BELOW: An orchard of apple trees includes vintage varieties such as Hewes Virginia Crab, Spitzenburg, Newtown Pippin, Baldwin, Cortland, and Golden Russet.

LOVE OF ESPALIER

Bunny softened the weathering stone walls with trees bent in forms of espalier, which is the training of a shrub or tree into a shape by fastening the branches to a wall or support. This imparted a beguiling appearance, especially when laden with ripened fruit in season.

Trees create added interest in a garden when trained against walls and shaped into different diagonal, upright, and horizontal patterns.

FLOWERS
AND EDIBLES

*"I am such an amateur at both gardening and writing
that some weeks I never know where to begin."*

On May 13, 1938, Bunny's article "Odds and Ends for May" was printed in the *Clarke Courier*.

"I am such an amateur at both gardening and writing that some weeks I never know where to begin. For instance, there is so much to be done in a garden this week and each subject, if properly explained, could take the entire amount of my allotted space, but as the things I am going to mention should all be done this week, please forgive the higgidy piggidy trend of thought.

"First, now is the time to plant all summer flowering bulbs: dahlias, gladiolas, montbretias, etc. For a succession of blooms plant Gladiolas at ten-day intervals. See that they are properly spaced at least four inches apart and five inches deep so that they will stand up during storms.

"It is still not too late to plant Dahlia seed of Coltness Hybrid, as they will flower in the late summer and be well worth the trouble. Keep Dahlias pinched back until July so as not to make too much top growth and they will have four or five buds near the base. Be sure they have plenty of room and are not crowded. Montbretias are a very lovely flower, that are not often seen, but are becoming more popular lately. They require the same treatment as Gladiolas. Speaking of Dahlias and Gladiolas, Mrs. Kenneth Levi sent

me some very good suggestions. Gladiolas will bloom several times if the part of the stem with the thin covering is left when you cut the bloom. I wish more people would write in experiences, for I appreciate it so much and it will be of interest to everyone. Also, when planting Dahlia tubers, they should be staked, so as not to injure the roots later, and a few ashes mixed in the soil at the time of planting helps the blooms. This Spring everything seems to have bloomed at once, and such things as Peonies and Iris, which usually carry the blooming season into June, are already at their height; therefore it is worthwhile sowing more annual seeds than usual.

"Sow annual seeds in between the Tulips and Peonies. Their foliage will help to shade the tiny annual seedlings from the hot midday sun until they are large enough to take care of themselves. Try some annuals that are entirely new to you, because this is the only way to vary your experience."

"It is now the season to prune your flowering shrubs without any hesitation and they will benefit greatly next season," she wrote in May 1938 for the *Clarke Courier*. "All dead wood is easily seen now and the older stalks should be thinned out from the bottom to allow the younger ones to develop. Lilac blooms must be cut off before they go to seed."

"As soon as the ground is dry enough, and that I must say seems a long way off at the moment, begin to plant a bed for Perennials, and Biennials. This should be in a partly shaded

OPPOSITE: When designing a border of flowers, Bunny worked alongside nature and often used the different shades and tints of color found in a single flower petal, creating scenes of beauty such as this.

ABOVE: Waves of Bunny's favorite blue Scillas were naturalized across the farmlands and meadows at Oak Spring. Scilla, an early spring-blooming bulb, is a member of the lily family.

ABOVE: Nature provided inspiration at every turn, as the wildflowers were allowed to roam freely.

OPPOSITE, ABOVE: Bunny's "pet" stone dog bearing a basket of blossoms seemed right at home in a corner of the garden amidst a cloud of spring blossoms.

OPPOSITE, BELOW: Blue was Bunny's favorite color—"all shades of blue." She planted flowers of this cool hue along garden paths, where their roaming habits lent their fairy-tale enchantment.

location although some sun is necessary during part of the day." She recommended "a corner in the vegetable garden," because the soil had "already been worked up and would need less preparation." Rake the soil very fine because the seeds are so small. And until the tender seedlings are established, "a covering of cheese cloth nailed to four corner posts will keep both heavy rains and sun from beating down on them."

The seeds should be sown in rows and labeled. "Thin them out so that each plant has sufficient space to develop," and in the fall, "transplant them to the place where you expect them to flower." Don't delay, she cautioned, because "the days become hot and dry and poor results are your reward." Perennials that "no garden should be without" included Delphiniums, Columbines, and Pyrethrum (painted daisies). "I do not want to seem unpatriotic," she implored, "but I have yet to see any of these plants grown from American seed that can measure up to the standard of those grown from English seed. I have planted both, but the comparison of English Perennials in both the size of the blooms, color and percent of good seed, is so far ahead that I cannot help but recommend them. Should you want to send for the catalogues, here they are: Sutton Seed Ltd., Reading, England; Dobbies, Edinburgh, Scotland."

OPPOSITE: Bunny eschewed tight plantings of flowers. Each flower, each limb, was to have its own space and be a good neighbor.

ABOVE: A panorama of beauty where nothing in particular can be noticed.

In the intervening years, the world went to war, resulting in disastrous personal consequences that contributed to the demise of Bunny's first marriage to Stacy Barcroft Lloyd, Jr., with whom she had two children: a son, Stacy III, and a daughter, Eliza. In 1948 she married widower Paul Mellon, the son of the American industrialist Andrew Mellon. Paul Mellon lived nearby at his farm, Oak Spring, in Fauquier County, where he bred thoroughbreds and fox hunted. He was an art connoisseur and philanthropist.

Vogue magazine gave their readers a narrow glimpse of the Mellons' lifestyle and a peek at Bunny's half-acre walled garden at Oak Spring in their July 1962 issue, "Mrs. Paul Mellon's Garden in Virginia." Casually dressed in a hat and gardening smock stitched by a friend, French courtier Hubert de Givenchy, Bunny permitted herself and her garden to be photographed—a rarity—while gazing at locust blossoms too high to reach and pruning lemon-colored nasturtiums in the greenhouse. *Vogue* understood Bunny's penchant for detail and described the scale of the garden as modest, "the detail superb, and the plants rather special—potted trees of standard thyme and rosemary grown in all sizes . . . cordons of apples and pears outlining flowers as well as vegetables . . . and in the greenhouse; rows of lemon and lime tree . . ." Other than that, the world would have to wait to see more.

OPPOSITE, ABOVE: Cordons of apple trees, underplanted with an assortment of cool-color flowers, stretch their limbs along a garden path of stone.

OPPOSITE, BELOW: A flower bed of white, with touches of warm colors, at the height of summer in the Cape Cod vegetable garden.

ABOVE: Steps to nowhere add atmosphere, especially when cloaked in the brilliance of summer.

EDIBLES

As space allows, fruit, herbs, and vegetables should be included in any garden plan, whether planted in a separate space or all together in a pleasing design. All will bring beauty and sustenance to the garden and table. A tomato ripened by the sun, herbs snipped from a little herb tree, or an apple plucked from a tree are nature's reward for tending a garden of one's own.

Fruit in all its ripened forms was readily available in the orchards during the harvest. Bunny built an Apple House at Oak Spring. There the cool-season crops were processed along a twenty-foot-conveyor belt before storage in refrigerated rooms, where the humidity and temperature could be controlled—ensuring plentiful year-round supplies of fruit at optimum flavor and texture.

The vegetable garden on the Lower Terrace at Oak Spring, freshly tilled and planted with vegetables in straight, orderly lines. Seeds for the red poppies were sent to Bunny from Gérald Van der Kemp, a French friend and art expert who masterminded the restoration of the palace at Versailles and, with Bunny's financial philanthropic support, Monet's garden at Giverny.

OPPOSITE AND ABOVE: At King's Leap, there were vegetable beds deemed as show gardens, where only the finest plants were displayed. These beds were covered with slatted structures to protect the precious plants from the strong island heat. A larger vegetable garden was located on a lower level at a distance from the house, where the water table was more plentiful.

RIGHT: A garden terrace with views of the bay below in the distance.

BUNNY'S LITTLE
HERB TREES

A garden's "greatest reality is not reality,
for it is always in a state of becoming."

From the time Bunny was a little girl traveling back and forth to school, she was deeply aware of the string of old apple trees that her father had transplanted along both sides of the driveway at Albemarle, her childhood home in Princeton, New Jersey. For her, they represented "stability and peace" and she knew "their shapes by heart." Springtime "came with blossoms and wild violets that crept into the grass around them" and were followed by the heavy shade of summer and "autumn's red and yellow apples." Winter was the most magical time of all, when the snow was streaked with blue shadows "that moved with the sun." Her fascination with trees grew from there.

Bunny became interested in growing standards, what she referred to as "little herb trees," when the gardener at George Washington's Mount Vernon shared a clipping from a myrtle tree with her. "These little herb trees, which recall the pure quality of a medieval monastery garden, began as an experiment to create something that would be to our culture, the culture of the Western Hemisphere, what the bonsai trees are to the Eastern; to produce a living plant that had the quality of an object."

Standards, by definition, are shrub-like plants that are trained to grow as a small tree with a straight stem. All shoots are pruned or pinched back, leaving only a topknot of growth. It was the perfect plant for a tree-lover like Bunny, who loved to prune. In fact, for her, pruning her little herb trees became an art form. "As it takes about two years to make and shape an herb tree, we keep adding to this collection. By now we have a small forest." Lucky were the friends who received one of these prized trees. "A pinched leaf of rosemary, thyme, or santolina will bring the scent of a country garden into any room; some friends who cook keep their trees in their kitchen where the trimming of the tree becomes the flavor of the stew."

Bunny found growing these little trees to be an "astonishment" that brought great joy for many years. She wrote that watching each one of them grow called on all the resources of the gardener, "who learns to live with faith, success, disappointment, and patience."

ABOVE: Bunny examining her little herb trees in her winter garden, the Formal Greenhouse at Oak Spring.

OPPOSITE: A brick masonry floor, sunken below the ground, is lined with her prized topiaries at Bunny's Lord and Burnham greenhouse at Oak Spring.

In December 1965, *Vogue* published Bunny's article "Green Flowers and Herb Trees," which she alluringly called, with tongue in cheek, the "mystery of true love." The article began with a rambling statement on the nature of gardening:

"Too much should not be explained about a garden. Its greatest reality is not reality, for a garden, hovering always in a state of becoming, sums its own past and its future. A garden, like a library, is a whole made up of separate interests and mysteries: among these mysteries are green flowers and the shaping of some herbs

ABOVE: A vignette assembled by Bunny with a few of her favorite things: a garden calendar, a myrtle topiary and an apple from one of her trees. She loved to create tableaux to sketch.

RIGHT: Herb trees potted in tubs flank the double-door entry into the central pavilion of the Formal Greenhouse.

OPPOSITE: Little herb trees displayed in the Oak Spring greenhouse (top) and the conservatory (bottom), a slat room that opened into the dining room at King's Leap.

ABOVE: Armies of little herb trees—thyme, rosemary, and santolina—were also grown in the working greenhouses at Rokeby Stables, which were also part of the Mellon farm in Upperville, Virginia.

OPPOSITE: A double-ball topiary tree graces the Upper Terrace at Oak Spring in autumn.

into small trees."

Green flowers are "enchanted flowers, magic flowers, the witches of the garden. They give an impression of reflected sunlight, the light of a Bonnard painting," with flowers that ranged from "the colors of emeralds to the color of moonlight on white flowers," and added a "secret formula of air and life" when mixed in with other colors.

There are two types of green flowers, some that "have always been green: the Ixia viridiflora; the long fringed orchid Platyclinis filiformis; the Cymbidium miretta, variety 'Glendessary',

grandparent of all green orchids; and the lacy Alchemilla major—the lady's-mantle, which is well known in England and, I think, not enough appreciated in America." And there are some that "suddenly become green: green zinnias, for instance, appeared unexpectedly among their family of wild, clear colors." The way to encourage this "serendipity," Bunny instructed, was to "protect and isolate the seeds." These "sports," the name for a part of a plant that differs from the rest of a plant, produced the tulip 'Artist', and nicotiana 'Lime'. "The lilies 'Green Dragon' and the 'Green Magic' strain resulted from careful, deliberate experiments, as did green auriculas."

"With the help of our inspired and scholarly gardener, Mr. Charles Pecora, and a greenhouse, we have green flowers all year. Neither in bouquets nor in flower beds do we use all green flowers together, for they deepen, brighten, and add subtlety to other colors. They have a mystery like true love that wants to hide but is betrayed by its own joy."

IN SUMMARY

"If once you fall under the spell of gardening,
of growing things . . . you will carry forever
a cure that will serve you well in life."

"Gardening takes patience, a reasonable amount of care, and a stout heart against disappointments. So, don't start out with ideas too big to be carried out. And don't let your enthusiasm or a nurseryman's enthusiasm carry you into a world that has no way out but a loss of temper and pocketbook. There are many excellent nurserymen and plantsmen who advise one on how to design. They don't mean to sell you a jungle when all you want is a pleasure garden. But they do. Their small obscure plants can grow into monstrous sizes and take over like unruly children. So ask how big they will grow. And be sparing in the beginning."

"The King's Kitchen Garden" was penned by Bunny in April 1993 as a foreword to *Versailles: The King's Vegetable Garden,* a book of photography of Potager du Roi by Jacques de Givry and Yves Perillon. In it she described her first visit to the garden with Hubert de Givenchy:

"It was many years ago that a friend took me, late one November afternoon, into the Potager du Roi. A light, damp mist veiled the garden as we entered through the door of a house on the north-east, the site of the original Figuerie. Being a gardener and a foreigner who for years had sought knowledge and collected books on the art of espalier it was an astonishing experience to be led into this garden of fruit trees trained against

~ 161 ~

walls and trellis, often reaching 20 feet in height. A few pears still clung to the trees, and wreaths of twigs, recently pruned, surrounded the standard varieties from which drops of water sparkled in the dusk. A solitary gardener passed, touching his cap. The silence, mystery and beauty were a gardener's equivalent to le Grand Meaulnes wandering into the lost domaine. My friend allowed me the pleasure of silent discovery . . . The garden had been an important element in the king's conception for Versailles, a part that would add to the perfection of his table and his extravagant manner of living and dining."

Bunny Mellon's last interview, "Bunny Mellon's Garden Secrets," was published in *Vanity Fair* in August 2010. James Reginato, who had been the lucky writer to receive her summons, quoted her: "Monday I'm planning my funeral, and Tuesday I've got Bette Midler. Come Wednesday at 11:30." In the article, Reginato insisted that, "indeed, throughout the second half of the 20th century, Bunny was widely venerated as the epitome of good taste and the true queen of Green, thanks to her prowess with gardens." He recapped her "career," which wasn't really a career at all but a passion for the things she loved, and served up a short and eloquent synopsis of Bunny's life, summarizing her friendships with Hubert de Givenchy and Jacqueline Kennedy, and—if you read between the lines—a kinship with Marie Antoinette, the famous French queen. "The greenhouse at Oak Spring would not be out of place at Versailles," Reginato charmingly noted.

Upon first stepping into Bunny's Oak Spring Garden, surrounded by cordons and espaliers of fruit trees, Antoine Jacobsohn, the current curator of le Potager du Roi and one who is exceptionally familiar with the gardening tastes of Queen Marie Antoinette, enthusiastically remarked, "Bunny Mellon has created her own American Hameau de la Reine!" Only in Bunny's case, "she escaped the protocol and pressure" with an attitude of "responsibility." And, chuckling, Antoine added, "I almost expect to see the Queen stroll around the corner."

What Bunny herself once said—and what became true of Jack Kennedy, Hubert de Givenchy, Marie Antoinette, Everett Hicks, Irvin Williams, and Perry Wheeler—"If once you fall under the spell of gardening, of growing things—of putting together colors, textures, forms, heights, materials—you will carry forever a cure that will serve you well in life."

A watercolor titled *Bunny's Garden*, painted by Mellon family friend Bee Dabney and featured in a little book she made for Bunny, *A Weekend in May*, 1964.

AFTERWORD

Randy Embrey

Former head gardener at Oak Spring

———

Five miles east of the Old Popular Tree atop Ashby's Gap, by the way the crow flies, is one of the grandest of all estates to ever adorn the Virginia Piedmont. Named Rokeby, the estate born of the vision of philanthropist Mr. Paul Mellon exemplifies the prominent standard of this fertile valley. Agrarian in foundation with her serene pastures, stands of white oaks bounded by ancient stone walls bestow a sense of magnificence upon one's linear sight. A slight upward gaze to the west, the Blue Ridge Mountains ripen softly into the skies, and to the east, the Bull Run Mountains stand astutely sheer with a faint smile of white. The convergence of Mr. Mellon's vision and nature's maturation was an experience to behold.

Facets of awe abound throughout every corner of Rokeby, and one I am particularly fond of is the quaint patch of ground known as the Oak Spring Garden. Oak Spring, the namesake of the primary residence of Rokeby, served as the minder of this patch. Protection from the elements of any given season, a dash of shade here or there, a pocket of warmth or a burst of light at a given moment created an inseparable marriage between home and garden.

The Oak Spring Garden was created by the hand of Mrs. Rachel "Bunny" Lambert Mellon. Mrs. Mellon, divinely gifted in the métier of circumstance and particularly in the arts of design, style, and taste, amongst others, had an unparalleled foresight of time and presence. She held the distinct ability to weave these divine gifts into the fabric of a sense of place to create her botanical masterpiece.

Simplistic in nature to the unassuming eye, the Oak Spring Garden unfolded at every turn, holding gifts not limited to a single sense but a full sensory experience and an invitation to reflect on seasonal shifts. The bones of the garden, lying naked and cold, exposed in their glory under the winter sky, gave honor to a bygone day whilst in the same moment gave hope of days to come. The walks of handmade bricks, their fading hues of crimson,

Early days at Oak Spring, before the Arbor
pathway was lined with 'Mary Potter' crab trees.

were adorned with emerald-colored moss. The paths of white gravel sprinkled with oyster shell tended to fade to perfection. The terrace of fieldstone with imperfect repose held the precise number of raindrops to quench a passing jaybird. A delinquent blossom of quince would occasionally appear as if unaware of its role in this season. Espaliered limbs, stretched with age, were now visibly on display, framing windows and searching for the unknown, crawling upon a whitewashed wall. Standing stately in the season of cold, apple trees pruned to perfection in and around the garden provided strength to the soul. Guardians of the garden, they were but botanical sculptures in this moment, a balance of natural shape and an artist's clay, pruned to perfection, not to resemble an egg, not to resemble an oval, not to resemble a sitting hen, somewhere in the unsaid place between; once achieved it was known.

Spring ushered in welcoming palettes of colors and smells, tulips born from a warming ground, with an occasional honeybee to dance with an infant petal. A crisp breeze carried a slight whiff of delicate lily of the valley. Rains came and went, with a lone snowflake gently falling upon the ground only to disappear as fast as it came. The cold winds defiantly surrendered to the inevitable passage of time. The archway connecting the garden and the Formal Greenhouse would now be at its zenith. The Mary Potter's blossoms of white gently blushed with a spattering of pink became a descending cloud of paradise. Heavy in bloom, petals in peak, bees at work created a tunnel of vibrational bliss, smells, and sights with the petals dropping as if confetti on a celebratory parade of victory. Tips of green sprouted from the frame of the trees, yellowing of foliage from a hardened winter gave in to tender

LEFT: Bunny makes a trip down memory lane and stands outside a garden shed that was used when she gardened as a young girl at her father's historic estate, Carter Hall, in Millwood, Virginia.

BELOW: The path on the north side of Bunny's Oak Spring Garden was covered with a mix of white pea gravel and oyster shells and lined with boxwood.

OPPOSITE: Trees, light, and shadow embellish the beauty of springtime on this walkway leading to the little house that Bunny called the School House. She was probably inspired by the School House at George Washington's garden at Mount Vernon.

life anew, and the evening air was alive with the old familiar chorus of the peeper frogs announcing spring was finally here.

The enticement of warmth gave the blessing of life, a renewal of hope, a sense of inspiration, intangible in feeling and tangible in form. The garden was alive, vegetables, flowers, shrubs, trees festooning upon the winter's bones into a vibrancy of botanical wonder. The warmth quite quickly turned to summer's heat, thus the cooling sounds of the flowing waters of the spillways and pools became now more prominent and pleasing than ever. The whitewashed walls surrounding the garden had a different appearance in the morning than in the late afternoon. Morning dew drew the veins of the greenstone walls into focus, while the day's heat took its toll in the afternoon, when the whitewash concealed the veins with its dry, chalky cloak. An occasional brass spike, mysteriously remaining from a bygone day, would often lend a faint trail of turquoise meandering down the wall. The herbaceous plants were at home, none shouting "look at me" but all united in communal cohesion. Structured but unstructured in nature, nothing was to be noticed as a specimen.

A stately oak left to its natural shape towered above all. Ornamental trees and shrubs were pruned and shaped in accordance to structure and style, as well as the cordons that were slightly elevated over the undergrowth of vegetation.

OPPOSITE: A riot of blossoms in one of Bunny's greenhouses at Oak Spring.

ABOVE: Bunny often mixed plants in gray and white tones into her planting schemes because she felt that they made the other colors pop and become vivid.

All plants were to be respected and all given an opportunity to have their space and their natural growth tendencies. Walled garden beds filled with plantings were often reminiscent of a deft Monet painting. The walkways were littered with plants in their cracks, mini French pinks, French strawberries, poppies, and violets, to name a few.

As the days grew shorter with summer coming to a close, the plantings often became a mere memory of their grandeur from months past. However, a beauty and lesson were here to behold. While color may have faded, the life coming to an end, there is beauty still. The story of the plant, its form and function, its past and present, its seed to be given to tomorrow, a decadence in death.

The death of summer is often marked by frost, and for many it's a gift from a long, hot summer. The change brings cool evenings, rustling winds, and colors so pervasive to the soul. In the garden the leaves have begun to fall—yellows, browns, reds litter the ground. Apples have come into season; birds head south as their songs become distant; smoke trickles from the solemn chimneys of Oak Spring. The gardens are put to rest, frosted by the mornings, warmed by the day's fading sun; they will soon wear the coat of winter. A time of reflection, a time of hope, and a time of rest. Such is life in the quaint patch of ground known as the Oak Spring Garden.

ABOVE: The main path in the Oak Spring Garden, which led from the back door of the house through the arbor and to the Formal Greenhouse, was framed in a profusion of lavender. Located nearby was a bed filled with varieties of mint, whose leaves were used in her special garden iced tea recipe.

OPPOSITE: The wall bed located at the north end of the garden planted in Bunny's soothing palette blooms forth like an impressionistic artist's dream.

OPPOSITE: What has become Bunny's trademark—a potted topiary—is one of two that stood as sentries on either side of the double gate that opened into the Oak Spring Garden.

ABOVE: The point of arrival at Oak Spring. The nondescript front door is located to the far left of this west-facing façade, which is decorated with an espaliered pear tree.

RIGHT: Paul and Bunny Mellon enjoyed walking their properties together. Here they pose for a rare photo, all bundled up at Oak Spring.

ACKNOWLEDGMENTS

We would like to thank the following people for their kind and generous support during the research, writing, and publishing of this tribute to Bunny and acknowledge their numerous contributions:

Nancy Collins for persevering with our research requests.

Anne and Gray Coyner for sharing local lore and history, warm beds, hospitality, and a delightful table.

Randy Embrey for so skillfully imparting Bunny's magic and wisdom.

Clay Helms for his technical expertise and patience.

Caroline Hoyt for her discriminating eye, discussions, and sharing her precious time.

Judy and Dick Kennedy for their warm Southern style hospitality.

Mellon Family Gardeners: Lisa Rockwell, Chris Harvie, Bob Hoxie, Laura Booth, Deborah Byrd, Kate Cliffton, Airynee Damewood, Desiree Lee, Wendi Sirat, and J. D. Tutwiler. Mellon estate stonemasons Bobby Childs and Tommy Reed.

Gwen Russell for lending her spiritual support.

P. Allen Smith and James H. Sumpter for their warmth, receptiveness, and beautiful words.

Draza Stamenich for his inspiration, hospitality, and photography.

Daniel Sutherland for sharing his sparkling photography that captured memorable moments.

Jacques de Givry for lending lovely photographs from his book, *The Gardens of Versailles*.

Rita Sowins for her beautiful book design.

Suzanne Gibbs Taylor and Madge Baird for giving us this spectacular opportunity.

The Gerard B. Lambert Foundation.

The Oak Spring Garden Foundation.

A lone basket waiting to be filled becomes a still life.

PHOTOGRAPHIC CREDITS

A hand drawing done by Bunny for her husband,
Paul Mellon. Her nickname for him was "Eléphant."

Jonathan Becker: front cover, 2, 6

Bee Dabney: 21, 163

Jacques de Givry: 26L, 27

"Horst P. Horst/Conde Nast Collection" via
Getty Images: back cover

Bob Hoxie: 102

John F. Kennedy Presidential Library: 37, 40, 41

Desiree Lee: 98T, 98B, 99

Bunny Mellon, © Thomas Lloyd, Gerard B.
Lambert Foundation: 1, 7, 11, 13, 17, 18, 26R,
28–31, 34, 35R, 44–52, 54–59, 62–65, 68–72, 73B,
74TL, 76–85, 87TR, 90, 91, 94–97, 101, 103, 105,
108, 110B, 111, 113–117, 119–121, 123–129, 131,
132B, 133, 136–151, 154–159, 165–171, 173B, 174,
175

Courtesy Oak Spring Garden Library: 38; eight
French school oil paintings, c. 1630: 14, 22, 42,
106, 134, 152, 160

Mark Peebler, courtesy Oak Spring Garden
Library: 53, 61, 89, 92, 93

Lisa Rockwell: 71, 73T

Draza Stamenich: 33T, 33B, 35L, 66–67, 88,
109R, 110T, 112L, 118T, 118B, 121B, 129LB, 130,
132T, 172, 173T

Daniel Sutherland: 74TR, 74BL, 74BR, 75, 86,
87B, 122T, 122B

First Edition

27 26 25 24   8 7 6 5

Published by

Gibbs Smith

P.O. Box 667

Layton, Utah 84041

1.800.835.4993 orders

www.gibbs-smith.com

Designed by Rita Sowins / Sowins Design

Printed and bound in China

Gibbs Smith books are printed on either recycled, 100% post-consumer waste, FSC-certified papers or on paper produced from sustainable PEFC-certified forest/controlled wood source. Learn more at www.pefc.org.

Library of Congress Control Number: 2020933160

ISBN: 9781423655404